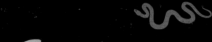

The Horse

Faster than the Wind

Valérie Tracqui

Photos by Gilles Delaborde

ini Charlesbridge

Mustangs are wild horses that live in the western United States.

In the desert

Desert rocks and sand bake in the summer sun. A small band of wild horses moves slowly over the dry land, searching for grass to eat.

A big male, called a stallion, suddenly lifts his head and listens intently as a prairie dog runs nearby. No danger threatens the band, so the stallion begins grazing again.

Hunger and thirst

The hot sun makes the horses thirsty. An old female, called a mare, leads the group to a stream. The horses walk in a straight line, one behind the other.

After the mare drinks, she rolls in the dust to scratch her coat. The other horses imitate her. They like the rough feel of the dirt.

Mustangs are always on the lookout for new pastures.

The horse drinks between ten and twenty gallons of water every day.

Because of its small stomach, the horse must eat all day to get enough food.

5

A hard hoof covers each foot.

Sensitive hairs surround the horse's mouth.

Whether it walks, trots, canters, or gallops, the horse likes to be on the move.

As healthy as a horse

A strong heart, big lungs, and powerful muscles help the horse run long distances very quickly without getting tired. Its long tail swats away annoying insects, and its brown, white, black, or gray coat helps the horse blend in with its surroundings. At the first sign of danger, the big animal gallops away as quickly as it can.

The horse can see in almost a full circle, but it relies mainly on hearing and smell to sense danger.

Among friends

Wild horses live in small groups, called family bands. Each horse automatically obeys a horse of higher rank.

The leader is the strongest stallion in the family. When an enemy threatens the band, he sounds the alarm and stays behind to fight until every member of the band has escaped.

The lead stallion stands lookout, always on the alert for danger.

The horse lays its ears back when it is angry or upset.

Horses love to nuzzle each other.

9

Young horses travel between full-grown mares for protection, while the lead stallion brings up the rear.

This antelope shares the Great Plains with the wild mustangs.

neighbors

Bands of wild horses also live on the prairie, alongside antelope, cows, and deer. When the horses gallop, the tall grass shakes under their thundering hooves. Prairie dogs quickly jump into their holes to hide until the larger animals have passed by.

Prairie dog holes are very dangerous. Stepping in one could break a horse's leg.

Mating season

In the spring, the wild horses are restless. It is mating season. Only the lead stallion is allowed to mate with the mares in his band. He guards them jealously and may fight younger males in his band or even the leaders of other groups if they come too close to the mares.

Sometimes several family bands gather together into a large herd and gallop across the prairie.

The lead stallion approaches and sniffs one of the mares to see if she will let him mate with her.

Droppings let other horses know that a stallion has passed this way.

This stallion calls a mare.

13

Birth

One day, a mare wanders away from the rest of the band. She lies down in the grass to give birth. When the baby, called a foal, is born, the mare licks it all over to clean and warm it. Before long, the foal tries to stand for the first time.

A mare is pregnant for eleven months.

A foal is born head and front feet first.

The foal must stay away from rattlesnakes. A bite on the nose could make it swell up, suffocating the baby horse.

As soon as it can stand, the foal looks for its mother's milk.

The foal gets tired very quickly. It rests in the grass while its mother grazes nearby.

15

Playmates

All the foals in the band like to run and play together, but they never stray very far from their mothers.

A mare teaches her foal to run from danger.

Even adult mustangs like to run together.

The foal begins to eat grass when it is one month old.

Two foals chase a butterfly across the prairie and jump over a river without noticing it. But when it is time to go back, the running water frightens them. The foals snort and whinny in fear, and their mothers rush to help them rejoin the band.

The mare watches her foal from the corner of her eye.

Three-year-old males play-fight to see which of them is the strongest.

All grown-up

The foals become adults when they are about two years old. Most of them leave their family band. Mares will be accepted by another band, but young stallions may start a band of their own. They try to steal mares from their leader or from another group, but lead stallions fight fiercely and often chase the younger males away.

Horses show their friendship by sniffing and nuzzling each other.

Horses often scratch each other's back with their sharp teeth.

19

Time to retire

One day, the lead stallion loses a fight. The winner chases ⸱m away from the ⸱ ⸱ e old stallion ⸱ ⸱ ⸱n other mares ⸱y to make friends ⸱ a younger male. ⸱⸱ ⸱ rse is a social an⸱ ⸱ ⸱ and hates to live by itself.

The new band leader mates with all the mares in the group. A year later, the mares will give birth again.

The smallest sound makes the mustangs restless. They are wild animals and do not like anything to come too close.

Taming the wild horse

Not everyone likes wild horses. Some people want to catch them and train them to work like domestic horses. Very few wild horses are still living free in the United States.

Ranchers capture wild mustangs with lassos.

Not truly wild

Almost all the wild horses in the United States today are domestic horses that have been released or have escaped from their owners. Some ranchers even allow their horses to grow up in nearly wild bands out in the country.

Safe at last

Mustangs are the descendants of horses that the first settlers brought to North America from Spain. Ranchers used to hunt wild horses to keep them from competing with livestock for food. In 1971 the United States passed a law to stop people from killing mustangs. Ranchers now capture and sell the horses or find people who will adopt them.

A wild horse that is captured but not adopted may spend the rest of its life inside a pen.

Looking ahead

Some people are trying to reintroduce wild horses into Mongolia, but in Australia, people still hunt them. Wild horses are becoming more and more rare in many countries around the world. Humans need to protect the last surviving wild horses before they disappear altogether.

To train a wild horse, a rancher must first let it get used to a bridle.

23

Cousins

The horse belongs to the same family as the donkey, the zebra, and the mule. They are all herbivores, which means they eat only plants. They all have hooves and love to gallop across wide-open spaces.

mule

The **mule** is a cross between a female horse and a male donkey. It is very strong and can live for sixty years, but female mules cannot have babies.

zebra

The **zebra** lives on the African savanna. Its tail is covered in skin with long hair only at the tip, and its mane is quite short. There are three different kinds of zebras. Each has a different stripe pattern and ear shape.

Przewalski's horse lives in Asia. Scientists believe that modern horses are descended from an ancient Przewalski's horse. Its coat is pale brown, and its muzzle is white. A black stripe links its bushy black mane to its tail.

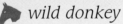 *Przewalski's horse*

wild donkey

The **wild donkey** often has striped legs and a black cross of hair on its back. Scientists believe that humans first caught and trained the wild donkey in Egypt about 8,000 years ago, well before the first wild horses were tamed.

25

A Quick Quiz about the Horse:

Photograph credits:
Jacques Delacour: p. 13 (top left); Philippe and Valérie Tracqui: p. 22 (bottom); A. Guerrier/Colibri: p. 23 (bottom); Gilles Delaborde: all other photographs.